POLITICAL
KILLINGS IN
NORTHERN
IRELAND

AI Index: EUR 45/01/94

ISBN: 1873328095

First published: February 1994

Amnesty International British Section
99-119 Rosebery Avenue
London
EC1R 4RE

This report was researched and written by Amnesty International's International Secretariat and all queries on the report should be directed to:Amnesty International International Secretariat, 1 Easton Street, London WC1X 8DJ. In accordance with the organisation's policy, Amnesty International British Section does not work on human rights violations in the United Kingdom.

Printed by Ennisfield Print and Design

Contents

Introduction

Current human rights concerns arise against a background of more than twenty years of civil conflict during which about 3400 people have been killed. The killings arising out of the civil conflict in Northern Ireland are not merely a result of armed encounters between armed political groups and the security forces: the picture is much more complex. In 24 years of conflict, since 1969, the largest number of deaths, over half, have been of civilians; almost a third of members of the security forces; and the rest are reported to have been members of armed political groups. The kinds of killings that fall within Amnesty International's mandate are threefold. They include killings by members of the security forces, killings by paramilitaries carried out with the acquiescence, collusion or complicity of the security forces, and deliberate and arbitrary killings by political groups.

In killings by security personnel in which the circumstances, but not responsibility, are disputed, the withholding or distortion of information may serve to conceal extrajudicial executions for which governments should be held accountable. Extrajudicial executions may also be concealed when deliberate killings are carried out by civilian paramilitary forces for which governments accept no responsibility, whenever such killings occur with the acquiescence, collusion or complicity of the security forces. Examination of investigative procedures and proceedings in particular incidents, and of the larger issue of essential safeguards for the prevention of extrajudicial executions, has been an essential part of Amnesty International's work on the United Kingdom. The monitoring of deliberate and arbitrary killings by armed non-governmental groups is also increasingly a focus of the organization's work.

Amnesty International has been investigating killings in disputed circumstances by members of the security forces in Northern Ireland for over a decade. The organization has focused in particular on those cases where it has been alleged that security force personnel deliberately killed people as an alternative to arresting them. A series of killings by the security forces in 1982 gave rise to serious allegations of an official policy of planned killings of suspected members of armed opposition groups. Subsequent killings in the next decade increased suspicions that such a policy existed. Amnesty International remains unconvinced by government statements that the policy does or did not exist because such statements are not substantiated by evidence of an official will to investigate fully and impartially each incident, to make the facts publicly known, to bring the perpetrators to justice or to bring legislation concerning such matters into line with international standards.

In recent years the organization has also been investigating collusion in political killings between members of the security forces and armed civilian groups, known as Loyalists in Northern Ireland, that support the continued union of Northern Ireland with Great Britain there. The victims of these killings have come from the minority Catholic community, and in particular those known for their activities in support of a united Ireland, commonly referred to as Republicans. Such collusion has existed at the level of the security forces and services, made possible by the apparent complacency, and complicity in this, of government officials. This element of apparent complicity has been seen, for example, in the failure of the authorities to take effective measures to stop collusion, to bring appropriate sanctions against people who colluded, or to deploy resources with equal vigour against both Republican and Loyalist armed groups that pursue campaigns of political murder.

Armed groups operate from both the Catholic and Protestant communities. The Republican armed opposition groups, notably the Irish Republican Army (IRA), come mainly from the Catholic community. They are opposed to the British presence in Northern Ireland and fight for a united Ireland. They are engaged in operations whose purpose, they affirm, is: a) to inflict heavy casualties on the security forces; b) to inflict major damage on the economic viability of Northern Ireland; and c) to undermine political stability. Members of the security forces are a prime target for the IRA, and they are at serious risk at all times including when they are unarmed, off duty and even retired. Others who have been victims of bombings and killings by Republican armed groups include: suspected members of Loyalist groups, suspected informers, and civilian personnel providing services to the security forces (including construction workers rebuilding bomb-damaged sites and canteen workers at police stations). The general public, too, is a target for bombings in public places (recently most deaths arising from such operations have been in London).

The paramilitary Ulster Defence Association (UDA) (which also acts under the name of the Ulster Freedom Fighters [UFF]), and the Ulster Volunteer Force (UVF) come from the Protestant community. They are known as Loyalists because they favour Northern Ireland remaining a part of the United Kingdom. The stated aim of their operations is to counter the Republican threat to the continued integration of Northern Ireland within the United Kingdom (UK) and this is done in part through intimidation and violence to crush support for Republican activities in Catholic areas. To this end, their activities include bombings and killings of suspected members of Republican armed groups as well as ordinary Catholics. In February 1992 a statement in the name of the UDA/UFF said that "those who aid and abet the Republican war machine, either by the ballot box or by other means, are deemed as guilty as those who pull the trigger". They also carry out shootings of alleged informers.

In a period of over 20 years the Republican armed groups have been responsible for over half the total number of deaths, the Loyalist groups for more than a quarter, and the security forces for about 11 per cent; in the past three years, however, Loyalist groups have carried out more killings than the IRA.

Both Republican and Loyalist groups also engage in "punishment" beatings, shootings and killings of members of their respective communities allegedly involved in "anti-social behaviour". The term "anti-social behaviour" has a very broad meaning, including alleged criminal activities, personal disputes and others.

Killings by members of the security forces

Between 1969 and November 1993, about 350 people were acknowledged to have been killed by members of the security forces in Northern Ireland. About half of the 350 were unarmed. Most of those killed came from the Catholic community. Many of these killings have been the subject of controversy through the years, because they happened in disputed circumstances.

Amnesty International's investigation began with three incidents of killings in late 1982 when six unarmed people were killed by members of a covert anti-terrorist squad within the Royal Ulster Constabulary (RUC, the Northern Ireland police force). Although prosecutions were brought concerning two of the deaths, no police officer was convicted. It emerged that senior police officers had concocted a false version of events and instructed policemen, under the Official Secrets Act, to give false testimony. As a result of public protest John Stalker, a senior British police officer, was appointed by the RUC Chief Constable in May 1984 to examine the cover-ups. He carried out his own re-examination of the evidence in all the cases and believed that he had uncovered crucial new evidence. He alleged that he was obstructed from carrying out a full investigation, and before it was completed he was removed from duty in suspicious circumstances. The inquiry was completed in April 1987 by Colin Sampson, a British Chief Constable. The findings of the Stalker/Sampson inquiry have never been published. In January 1988 the Attorney General announced that the inquiry revealed evidence that RUC officers had attempted or conspired to pervert the course of justice. Nevertheless because of "national security" and "public interest" considerations, no officer was prosecuted. Disciplinary hearings resulted in 18 officers being reprimanded and one cautioned.

The only alleged criminal actions referred to by the government concerned perverting the course of justice.

However, John Stalker had stated that he had uncovered new evidence about the incidents which could point to unlawful killings by policemen in all six deaths. Moreover, a BBC program entitled Public Eye reported that Colin Sampson had himself recommended in 1987 that some RUC officers be prosecuted on criminal charges, including conspiracy to murder one of those killed in 1982. It was also reported that he recommended charges be brought against MI5 (intelligence) officers for the deliberate destruction of a surveillance tape-recording of the shooting of Michael Tighe (crucial evidence in determining whether unlawful action had been taken). Nothing was ever divulged by the government concerning the new evidence uncovered by the inquiry; however at an inquest into one of the incidents, which began in May 1992, the coroner stated his intention of having this evidence presented. To date this evidence has not yet been heard.

The new evidence uncovered by John Stalker has been in the possession of the Northern Ireland Director of Public Prosecutions (DPP) since 1987. It is not known whether or not the DPP considered further criminal prosecutions in relation to the incidents. However, Amnesty International believes that the failure to bring prosecutions in connection with the killings resulted in a concealment of evidence of possible unlawful actions of state officials. Furthermore, the failure to bring prosecutions for the destruction of the tape suggests that the government condoned the deliberate destruction of evidence in a potential murder case.

Certain conclusions may be drawn about the 1982 incidents from the Stalker inquiry and its aftermath. It was clear that suspected members of Republican armed groups who were under surveillance were killed, while unarmed, by a covert anti-terrorist squad of the RUC, and that the surveillance operations involved a large number of police and intelligence officers. The original police investigations were deeply flawed; some officers conspired to cover up the truth; an external police inquiry was allegedly hampered by further attempts to cover up the truth; the failure to publish the findings of the inquiry or to prosecute police officers for alleged offences led to covering up the truth; and the repeated measures to conceal the truth contributed to what was effective immunity from prosecution, and possible impunity for murder.

In many other instances where security force personnel allegedly killed rather than arrested people, the justifications given by security personnel have been identical: either that a person appeared to reach for a gun and so was shot in self-defence or that the driver of a car drove through a roadblock (sometimes allegedly hitting a soldier or policeman) and that the car was fired at subsequently. In the killing of three unarmed IRA members in Gibraltar in 1988 the soldiers testified to an inquest that the suspects appeared to be about to trigger a hidden remote control detonator (although no such device was found on their bodies). Kevin McGovern, a 19-year-old student who had no paramilitary connections and who was killed in 1991, "appeared" to have thrown something at the police. It was claimed that Martin Peake, 17, and Karen Reilly, 18, who were driving round in a stolen car (known as "joyriding"), were shot dead after driving through an army checkpoint and hitting a soldier. It has been shown in a number of cases that the official version of events was untrue.

After the outcry over the 1982 incidents, the main responsibility for covert operations returned to the British Army, which has to a large extent been autonomous in security matters despite formal police primacy in Northern Ireland. In almost all the disputed incidents involving the security forces since 1982 the main protagonists have been soldiers.

Between 1976 and 1992, soldiers from the army's elite Special Air Services (SAS) regiment killed 37 reported members of the IRA (reportedly there have not been any SAS actions against Loyalist paramilitaries). The SAS is used for planned ambushes and there are repeated allegations that its policy is not "to take prisoners". The question raised is whether the security forces, having been tipped off about an impending action, could not in some cases have arrested the paramilitaries, whether efforts to surrender were made but disregarded, or whether opportunities to surrender were given to suspects, armed or unarmed, who were facing overwhelming military force.

One example of a planned operation was the ambush of eight IRA men, who were engaged in bombing a police station in Loughgall village in 1987. As they opened fire on the police station, they were shot at by well-positioned SAS troops overlooking the area and using machine guns. According to a journalist, Mark Urban, a senior security forces officer who played a key role in the operation told him: "Loughgall was a plum -it was an exceptionally heavy team of good operators. The temptation was there to remove them in one go. The terrorists played into our hands and everything went our way. Was it a decision to kill those people: I don't think it would have been phrased like that. Somebody would have said, `How far do we go to remove this group of terrorists?' and the answer would have been, `As far as necessary'."

In a recent book on undercover operations[1], Mark Urban concluded that government authorities, in dealings with the press, courts and Parliament, usually tried to represent SAS ambushes as the result of chance encounters in which people were killed only because the soldiers believed themselves or others to be in imminent danger, but that in reality the SAS was used quite deliberately to kill on ambush missions. He said that his research uncovered evidence that the usage of informers sometimes resulted in unlawful actions. He also uncovered many instances of the army and police deliberately giving the press false information about covert operations. Tom King, the former Secretary of State for Northern Ireland, said in 1990 that the authorities used disinformation to protect lives and for "absolutely honourable security reasons". Mark Urban further observed that the courts were routinely deceived by the security forces.

In February 1985 three IRA men were killed by the SAS while returning weapons to a cache after an aborted attack on police officers. At the inquest it was stated that an army patrol had encountered the armed men in a field and had opened fire after the three had pointed guns at them. It was denied that the soldiers had known of the planned IRA attack in advance. A pathologist testified that one of them had been hit by at least 28 bullets, most of them fired as he lay on the ground and that all three had single gunshot wounds to the head. The discrepancies between soldiers' and police testimony suggested that the security forces had known of the IRA attack in advance, and supported the allegations that the SAS ambush was planned from the start to kill the suspects regardless of the immediate threat or absence of a threat posed by them.

SAS soldiers were also involved in the killing of Seamus McElwaine, an IRA member, in April 1986. He was one of two men fired at by the undercover soldiers as they walked across a field to inspect a bomb. They were both armed. The other man, Sean Lynch, was slightly wounded and managed to hide for several hours before his arrest by British Army soldiers from a conventional unit. He alleged that after Seamus McElwaine had been initially wounded, he had been questioned and then shot again. The jury at an inquest hearing in January 1993 decided that the two men had not been challenged, that McElwaine had been wounded in an initial burst of gunfire and that while incapacitated and in the custody of the soldiers, he had been questioned, after which he had been shot dead. The DPP called for a full police report, in light of the inquest jury findings; however, by the end of November no decision had yet been made as to whether prosecutions should be brought.

The pattern that has emerged, and that causes concern, is one of repeated allegations that suspects are arbitrarily killed rather than being arrested, that members of the security forces believe they can operate with impunity, and that this is reinforced by government failure to take steps to prevent unlawful killings. The government evades responsibility by hiding behind an array of legal procedures and secret inquiries which serve to cloud the issues. These issues are: whether there is a policy at any official level to kill government opponents rather than to detain them (this includes allegations of collusion between the security forces and Loyalist armed groups), whether legislation acts as an effective deterrent to unlawful killings, whether disputed incidents are thoroughly and impartially investigated and whether perpetrators of unlawful killings are brought to justice.

Amnesty International's approach in examining disputed killings has been the following:
a) to monitor investigative procedures used in individual incidents to assess whether all the facts have been made known;
b) to compare legislation and its application with international standards;
c) to monitor government action;
d) to assess the facts of each case as they emerge.

Investigative Procedures: practice and standards

The procedures used to investigate disputed killings in Northern Ireland are ineffective in establishing all the facts and in making them public. In some cases evidence has shown that police investigations may have been deliberately superficial in order to protect security force personnel. In response to the Stalker/Sampson report, the RUC agreed that all further killings by the RUC would be investigated by an outside police force. This has not in fact happened in any single subsequent case. Killings by British Army soldiers, too, are investigated by the RUC. In July 1991 Amnesty International requested information on procedures for interviewing soldiers involved in killings as contrasted with those in force for police officers or civilians, but did not receive a reply. Furthermore, members of the security forces involved in disputed killings have rarely been suspended pending police investigation.

The investigation of such incidents is subject to particular delays by the length of time taken by the DPP in making decisions concerning possible prosecutions. For example, Brian Robinson, a UVF member, was killed by undercover soldiers in September 1989 and the DPP's decision not to prosecute was only made known in October 1991. John McNeill, Edward Hale and Peter Thompson were shot in January 1990 by undercover soldiers and the DPP's decision not to prosecute was made known two years later. The delays in holding inquests (of up to eleven years - see below) are also of concern.

Between 1969 and 1991, 21 members of the security forces were prosecuted for killings using firearms while on duty in Northern Ireland. Nineteen were found not guilty and one was convicted of manslaughter and given a suspended sentence. Just one — a soldier — was convicted of murder. Although given a life sentence, he was released after serving two years and three months of his sentence and reinstated in the army.

More recently prosecutions have been brought in four incidents. In July 1991 six British Army soldiers were charged in connection with the killing of two joyriders, Martin Peake and Karen Reilly, in a stolen car; in February 1992 a murder charge was brought against two soldiers for the killing in his car of Fergal Caraher; in

June 1992 an RUC officer was charged with the murder of Kevin McGovern; and in April 1993 two soldiers were charged with the murder of Peter McBride.

The trial of six British Army soldiers, charged in connection with the killings of Karen Reilly and Martin Peake, began in March 1993. Karen Reilly and Martin Peake were shot dead in September 1990 while in a stolen car. One soldier was charged with the murder of Karen Reilly, two with attempting to murder Martin Peake, and all six with attempting to pervert the course of justice and with obstructing the police investigation into the shooting. The soldiers of the 3rd Parachute Regiment had been on patrol with an RUC officer, whose evidence proved to be crucial in the case. The soldiers claimed that the stolen car appeared to drive at one of the soldiers and that this was their justification for opening fire. However, the police officer gave evidence that he had not seen the car endangering any soldiers. He also testified that after the shooting he heard the soldiers confer and then saw one soldier appearing to injure another. In the end, one soldier was found guilty of the murder of Karen Reilly; and one soldier of the attempted murder of Martin Peake and perverting the course of justice.

However, prosecutions have not been brought in a number of recent cases where the circumstances were highly suspicious, and in particular in cases where the killings were carried out by members of undercover army or police units. Such cases include the killing of John McNeill, Edward Hale and Peter Thompson in 1990, Brian Robinson in 1989, and Pearse Jordan in 1992.

RUC officers shot dead Pearse Jordan, who was later confirmed to be an unarmed IRA member, on 25 November 1992. The circumstances of the killing suggested that it might have been a pre-planned operation to kill rather than arrest him. Security sources initially claimed in unofficial statements to the press that they were in pursuit of Jordan's car as he drove towards the city centre when he rammed them; that gloves and masks were found in his car; that he was shot running away; that a second man was arrested at the scene; that an explosive device linked with the killing was found nearby; and that he was a former remand prisoner.

However, eyewitnesses stated that after two unmarked police vehicles forced his car off the road and boxed him in, Jordan got out of his car and started to run across the road. There was then a burst of gunfire from one of the officers. One eyewitness stated:

"The police got out [of the car] just as quick as he did. They could have caught him. There was no warning whatsoever, they opened up right away."

The post-mortem examination found that he had been shot by two bullets in the back, and a third in the back of his left arm. In addition it was reported that no masks or gloves or explosives were found, that no one was arrested and that Jordan had never been imprisoned. The initial claims which security sources hastened to make after the shooting appeared to be no more than a cover story tending to justify the killing. The police officer responsible for the killing was removed from active duty and given office work pending the police investigation into the incident. The investigation was carried out by a senior RUC officer from outside Belfast, and was completed by May 1993. In November the DPP announced that prosecutions would not be brought.

The family alleged that prior to his killing Pearse Jordan had been threatened on several occasions by RUC officers and soldiers, and that ten days before the shooting a soldier had taken a photograph of him at an army checkpoint. The family have submitted an application to the European Commission on Human Rights, claiming that Pearse Jordan has been unlawfully killed.

A further problem in deterring unlawful action by the security forces lies in the charges permitted by law. Soldiers or police officers considered to have killed someone in the line of duty must be charged with murder and not manslaughter. The requirements for proving murder are particularly high and a sentence of life imprisonment is mandatory. Courts are often reluctant to bring in the murder verdict in such situations. Members of the legal profession have made a number of suggestions for altering the law in such cases, by bringing in a middle charge.[2]

Since court proceedings involving the prosecution of security force personnel for disputed killings are rare, one of the main mechanisms for investigating suspicious deaths has been the coroner's inquest. In previous documents Amnesty International has written extensively about the main features of inquests which obstruct the victims' families from obtaining the full facts, including the lack of a final verdict, the refusal of security personnel to testify, the lack of legal aid, and the non-disclosure in advance of forensic and witness statements.[3]

During the first half of 1993 a number of inquests took place into the deaths of people killed by the security forces. Although these inquests revealed some information about the incidents, given the restrictions on the inquests the full circumstances of the killings were not made known. Amnesty International was also particularly concerned by the government's issuing of Public Interest Immunity Certificates (PIICs) which block the disclosure of crucial information concerning the planning of operations.

In January an inquest examined the circumstances of the killing of Seamus McElwaine, an IRA member and escaper from the Maze prison. He was shot dead in April 1986 by SAS soldiers, as he was walking across a field to inspect a bomb. He was armed at the time. The SAS soldiers did not testify to the inquest; only the commander of the SAS unit testified, speaking from behind a screen. Before the inquest opened, the government issued a PIIC preventing disclosure of some details relating to the army's undercover operation. The jury ruled that undercover soldiers had opened fire without giving Seamus McElwaine a chance to surrender, although that statement was later withdrawn after it was stated that the jury could not issue an opinion. The jury also decided that he had been wounded in an initial burst of gunfire, and that while incapacitated and in the custody of the soldiers he had been questioned, after which he had been shot dead. The coroner at the inquest, on hearing evidence by the surviving IRA member Sean Lynch (see page 7 of this report), said: "If what you say is correct, that would have to be cold-blooded murder".

In March an inquest heard evidence about the killing of three IRA members, Gerard and Martin Harte and Brian Mullin, by the SAS in August 1988. None of the SAS members directly involved in the shootings were present at the inquest; their written statements were read out as evidence. Other evidence was withheld by the government which issued PIICs to prevent disclosure. The jury was told that more than 200 bullets were fired by the SAS, who admitted that no warnings had been given before firing. The SAS claim that the three had opened fire first was not accepted by the jury who found that the evidence was inconclusive on who had fired first.

Another inquest in March examined evidence concerning the killing of Aidan McAnespie in February 1988. He was shot dead by a British soldier while walking through a border checkpoint. The soldier claimed that his hands were wet and accidentally slipped onto the trigger of a machine gun he was holding. The jury returned a finding that the soldiers in charge of the checkpoint were guilty of contravening standing orders in relation to the handling of weapons because the fatal shot had come from a machine gun which was cocked and ready to fire.

The inquest into the deaths of John McNeill, Edward Hale and Peter Thompson began in April; the three were killed by undercover soldiers in January 1990. The inquest was adjourned after legal challenges by the Crown to the Coroner's decision not to accept the Crown's claim that PIICs would apply to oral evidence; or that they could be used to justify the screening of soldiers while giving evidence. The government insisted that the soldiers should be allowed to testify behind specially erected screens in the interests of national security and to protect their lives and their families and not jeopardize future intelligence and undercover operations by the army. According to the High Court judgment issued in June 1993, the coroner had erred in law concerning the Certificates; the judge stated that the coroner should attach due weight to their contents. The deceased's families have appealed the High Court decision.

At the end of the inquest in June into the death of 17-year-old Gerard Maginn, the parents said that there were still "unanswered questions" about the circumstances of his death. He was shot dead when the RUC fired on a stolen car in which he was a passenger in November 1991. The RUC's claim, that their officers were involved in a high-speed car chase during which shots were fired, was contradicted by eyewitnesses. The inquest jury concluded that a police officer had walked up to the car, shouted a warning and tried to smash the window with his revolver butt. As he did so, the car reversed at speed towards one of their cars and officers "believing themselves to be under increasing threat" had opened fire. Gerard's mother said that the evidence did not reflect the image of frightened policemen who had opened fire in panic: "How a highly trained man who thought his life was in danger walked up to a car and hit it with the butt of his gun - to me that was not the action of someone who thought his life was under threat." Family members also expressed concern about the immediate investigative procedures after the killing because the RUC officers involved had been reportedly left together and alone before being questioned by senior officers.

The investigative procedures in Northern Ireland do not meet the minimum standards for proper investigations of disputed killings, as laid out by the United Nations Special Rapporteur on summary or arbitrary executions[4] in January 1988. The procedures also contravene the United Nations Principles on the Effective Prevention and Investigation of Extra-Legal, Arbitrary and Summary Executions, adopted by the UN Economic and Social Council in May 1989.

The UN Special Rapporteur noted in his January 1988 report the **minimum elements** of standards for proper investigations into all cases of suspicious death. These include: promptness, impartiality, thoroughness, and publication of the findings of the investigation. They also state that the family of the victim and lawyers should be able to participate in the investigatory proceedings and have access to substantive information at various stages of the investigation.

The Use of Lethal Force: Laws and Regulations/ International Standards

The laws and regulations applied in Northern Ireland which govern the use of lethal force by security forces are inadequate to prevent and deter unlawful killings. The regulations governing the actions of the RUC (Force Instructions) and the army (the "yellow card") are secret documents, thus evading public scrutiny. There is also a discrepancy between the law as applied in Northern Ireland and relevant international legal standards. International standards, such as Article 2(2) of the European Convention on Human Rights, speak of "absolute necessity" and "strict necessity" to justify deprivation of life. The Criminal Law Act (Northern Ireland) 1967 states that "such force as is reasonable in the circumstances" may be used to prevent crime. The law does not refer specifically to the use of lethal force.[5] Amnesty International believes that the concept of "reasonable" use of force is too flexible both to impose standards of behaviour on security forces which prevent excessive use of lethal force and to deter excessive force. This conclusion arises mainly from a review of court interpretations of the law; these established norms which fall short of the test of absolute or strict necessity. It is also reinforced in the light of the very few cases of disputed killings in which members of the security forces have been prosecuted and convicted.

Amnesty International sought clarification in 1991 on what steps the government has taken to bring international standards to the attention of various official bodies within the United Kingdom, and in particular in Northern Ireland. The organization asked whether the government was considering formulating appropriate legislation and policy directives in order to implement the UN Basic Principles on the Use of Force and Firearms by Law Enforcement Officials. No reply to these questions has been received.

Amnesty International has called upon the government to ensure that disputed killings are dealt with impartially, that the full truth about these killings is made known, and that all perpetrators of unlawful actions are brought to justice. As a means to this end, it has called for an independent judicial inquiry to review all the disputed killings by security forces since 1982 with a view to establishing procedures which would ensure that such incidents are impartially investigated and that the full facts are made public. This inquiry should also review the effectiveness of current legislation in providing clear guidance on the circumstances in which the use of lethal force is permissible and in deterring unlawful killings by members of the security forces.

Collusion between security forces and armed groups

The Stevens Inquiry 1989-90

In August 1989 UDA/UFF spokesmen justified their killing of a Catholic, Loughlin Maginn, by saying that he was an IRA member, and that this information was based on police files. Within weeks it was confirmed that security documents had gone missing from two security bases. As a result of the public outcry, the Chief Constable of the RUC appointed John Stevens, a senior British police officer, to investigate these security leaks in what became known as the Stevens inquiry. By the end of September 1989 lists containing over 250 names of suspects from police files had been leaked to the media or copies pasted on Belfast street walls. These were security force documents and included pictures, names, addresses, car registration numbers and sometimes other details about Republican suspects' movements. It was alleged that such documents were regularly handed over by members of the security forces to Loyalist armed groups, who had allegedly used them in some cases to target individuals and kill them.[6]

Nineteen people were killed by Loyalist groups in 1989 and the same number in 1990, but in 1991 the toll sharply increased to 41, and in 1992 to 34.

Two Ulster Defence Regiment (UDR) soldiers were charged in 1989 with the murder of Loughlin Maginn. One soldier stated he had the victim under surveillance on six occasions while on duty - going to his home to identify him, checking the car outside the home and noting his movements. Both UDR soldiers were given life sentences in March 1992 for passing on information which led to the killing of Loughlin Maginn. The soldier stated that he had also passed on the names of 14 suspects to the then legal UDA, had followed some of them and gathered information for the UDA while on duty, and had passed ammunition on to the UDA.

A summary of the report of the Stevens inquiry, which set out 83 recommendations, was released in May 1990. As a result of the inquiry, 59 people were charged or reported to the DPP. The offences for which charges were brought centred almost exclusively on the mishandling of classified intelligence documents: they included the unlawful possession of documents and communicating them to others without authorization, and collecting and recording security information. Some charges were also brought for firearms offences. The overwhelming majority, 32 of those arrested, were members of Loyalist organizations. No one was charged with conspiracy to murder except for one UDA officer, whose role had become notorious - because he was an army agent. This was Brian Nelson (see below). The Stevens inquiry summary noted that "in the present climate" in Northern Ireland leaks of official security information "may never be completely eliminated". However, it stated that measures already taken had reduced the opportunity for such leaks; and that "the passing of information had been restricted to a small number of individuals". The inquiry failed to identify members of the security forces involved in passing on information to Loyalist armed groups. It also clearly failed to enjoy the full cooperation of the British Army - had it done so, the facts which emerged about its agent Brian Nelson might have been more complete.

Amnesty International monitored these developments because it was concerned about allegations that members of the security forces used their official status to target suspected members of opposition groups for murder. The Stevens inquiry would have been very important if its scope had been wide enough to look at the issue of collusion as a whole, but unfortunately the inquiry was limited to leaks of security documents at the time and other related issues. It did not look at evidence that collusion between members of the security forces and Loyalist armed groups had been going on for many years, or at the overall pattern as it related to both targeted and random killings of Catholics. It did not examine the authorities' record during this time in bringing criminal proceedings against security personnel in this regard, or the official response to evidence of partiality and discriminatory treatment, for example, soldiers shouting verbal abuse at Catholics or writing sectarian graffiti on walls.

The Case of Brian Nelson

Brian Nelson was one of the UDA leaders arrested as a result of the Stevens inquiry. He was an agent of the army's Military Intelligence service who also served from 1987 to 1990 as the senior intelligence officer of the UDA. He had been associated with the UDA since 1972, and had also worked within the UDA for Military Intelligence from 1983 to 1985.

Brian Nelson's arrest was the most significant outcome of the inquiry. Shortly before his trial,[7] however, the most serious charges against him were dropped. The prosecution explained that it had dropped 15 charges, including two charges of murder, "after a painstaking and scrupulous assessment of possible evidential difficulties with the prosecution, and a rigorous examination *of the interests of justice*" [our emphasis].

A consequence of the accommodation between the prosecution and the defence, in which only one witness (an anonymous army official usually referred to as Colonel 'J') was called and cross-examination was almost entirely dispensed with, was a trial in which only fragments of the truth bearing on allegations of collusion emerged. The prosecution failed to probe fully the extent of Brian Nelson's knowledge and involvement in the UDA's criminal actions or the behaviour of Military Intelligence, which used him as an agent. Nor did the prosecution probe the peculiarly passive nature of the security forces' attitude towards the UDA, despite its repeated characterization by the prosecution in the course of the trial as a "terrorist" organization engaged in "murderous activities" (the UDA was at that time a legal organization).

Brian Nelson pleaded guilty to 20 charges, including conspiracy to murder five named individuals and collecting and possessing information likely to be of use to terrorists. All of the charges were based on his actions as the top intelligence officer of the UDA. He was said to have held primary responsibility for gathering and disseminating intelligence on suspected Republicans, including the conduct of surveillance operations and targeting for UDA "death squad" operations, even though he was at the same time an agent of Military Intelligence. As such he provided UDA intelligence reports on Republican suspects to his army controllers and informed them of UDA surveillance operations and their findings, and of plans to kill specific individuals.However, it was reported in a television documentary[8] that his warnings saved the lives of only two individuals, and led neither to arrests nor to raids on UDA operations. His military controllers, in addition, are alleged to have assisted in the production of photographs and other information used to target other Republican suspects for murder. It has also been alleged that Brian Nelson played a vital role in at least ten murders, attempted murders and conspiracies to murder; and that he targeted another 16 people who were later murdered, or against whom murder attempts were made. Brian Nelson reportedly distributed copies of the UDA file cards on suspects to at least five people within the UDA, as well as to another Loyalist paramilitary organization, the UVF.

Colonel 'J', a top military intelligence officer, testified to the trial on behalf of Brian Nelson. It was clear from his testimony that Brian Nelson was considered to be a very important agent. According to him, Brian Nelson brought UDA material to the army on a weekly basis. Files copied to the army included official photo-montages of Republican suspects that had been leaked to the UDA, other reports from all sectors of the security forces, as well as intelligence information gathered by the UDA. In the beginning of Nelson's assignment in 1987, Military Intelligence acknowledged having taken the entire set of UDA files into its temporary possession; it is alleged, moreover, to have streamlined the UDA's records and targeting system at that time, making the files more accurate and up-to-date and weeding out the file cards of non-Republican suspects. Colonel 'J' stated that the information coming from Brian Nelson was shared with the RUC, including the Chief Constable. It was clear, then, that the army and the RUC were aware of the flow of their own intelligence reports to the UDA, and their use in targeting suspects for killings, at least as early as May 1987. Intelligence material gathered by the UDA on Republican suspects, in turn, may have facilitated security force operations targeting Republicans: a way in which the UDA's civilian network augmented the military's own intelligence apparatus. Nor were the claims explored that Military Intelligence had passed on information on potential targets to the UDA via Brian Nelson.

Nothing in the evidence presented to the court indicated that the early knowledge of the extensive collection of security documents in the hands of the UDA resulted in steps to tighten procedures to stop the flow of intelligence information to the UDA. Nor was the larger issue of the failure to undertake the wholesale suppression of what the colonel described as the UDA's "murderous activities" addressed before the court; rather, the army's efforts as described to the court aimed exclusively at pre-empting certain individual planned killings. The evidence from the few individual cases of conspiracy to murder for which charges were brought suggest that Brian Nelson, and by extension Military Intelligence, were aware of the identities both of UDA leaders at the planning and policy level, as well as individual gunmen.

The apparent failure of the security forces to take significant action against UDA "death squads", however, was not addressed before the court and remains unaddressed. The court did not hear of a single arrest, or interception operation, carried out on the basis of information provided by Brian Nelson. Although it is clear that some arrests of Loyalist gunmen did occur during this period, these were neither large in number nor of people high in rank within the UDA.

Judge Kelly queried the apparent failure to prosecute UDA members responsible for the crimes Brian Nelson was intended to prevent:
"Were any of these men prosecuted for murder, conspiracy to murder? I've dealt with some of them, but only on lesser charges, the possession of documents."
Defence counsel's response was simple: *"He has never been asked to give evidence on these people"* [our emphasis]. The judge continued the same line of questioning on the apparent impunity of those working with Brian Nelson within the UDA. He said he recalled "two names of people prosecuted for collecting information" whom he had dealt with earlier that year, "Other than that, others were not charged with any crime." Defence counsel responded that this was "through no fault of Brian Nelson, who gave detailed evidence and his full cooperation".

Even more serious is the allegation that the army failed to intervene to save lives in many instances. Although Colonel 'J' assured the court that information about many planned attacks was passed on to the RUC, this was vigorously denied by the then RUC Chief Constable, who claimed they received limited information.[9] In fact, even in the cases cited in Brian Nelson's defence, the RUC reportedly maintained they had not been informed of attacks in advance. In the case of the killing of solicitor Patrick Finucane, Brian Nelson reportedly informed his army controllers of the planned murder two months in advance, but according to the RUC no message was passed on to it. The army controllers were also aware that another solicitor, Patrick McGrory, was being targeted. However, Patrick McGrory only received a warning three months after Brian Nelson was arrested, and the police allegedly had had difficulty extracting information from the army. The RUC said it was not informed of the warning that IRA member Brendan Davison, who was also an RUC agent, was being targeted by the UDA, although it is believed that Military Intelligence was aware of his dual role. He was subsequently killed. It was further reported that, although warned, the army failed to intercept a major arms shipment from arms suppliers in South Africa to the Loyalist armed groups (from which some of the weapons are still in regular use).[10]

Colonel 'J's testimony seemed not to take into account the evidence that Brian Nelson was, while perhaps loyal to the army, also an active advocate of the cause pursued by the UDA "death squads" and an active participant in their work. The possibility that loyalty to the army was not, in this case, wholly contradictory to a continuing loyalty to the UDA and the cause of the Loyalist paramilitaries, cannot be discarded. As characterized by Colonel 'J': "His motivation was to make his community safer, to bring down the terrorist organizations". To the UDA, however, the term "terrorist organizations" may apply only to the Republican organizations to which they claim to react.

Brian Nelson was sentenced to three years' imprisonment on each of 11 counts of possession of documents likely to be useful to terrorists, six years' imprisonment on one count of possession of firearms with intent to endanger life, and 10 years on each count of conspiracy to murder. The sentences are concurrent.

The Killing of Patrick Finucane

Patrick Finucane, aged 39, was a prominent criminal defence and civil rights lawyer; his was one of the leading law firms acting in defence of those detained and/or charged under emergency legislation in Northern Ireland. He was shot dead by two masked men on 12 February 1989 in front of his wife and three children, aged 9, 13 and 17. His wife was also injured during the attack. The killing was claimed in the name of UDA/UFF, which said that Patrick Finucane had been "an IRA member". This claim was denied both by family and friends, and in public statements by the police.

At the inquest into his death it was stated that he had been struck by 14 bullets to the head, neck and trunk. At least one of the bullets fired into his head was fired from a range of 15 inches. Detective Superintendent Simpson of the RUC stated: "His murder was unusual both for its ferocity and the fact that he was struck by all 14 shots fired." One of the weapons used in the attack had been one of 13 weapons stolen from British Army barracks in 1987 by a member of the Ulster Defence Regiment (a local British Army regiment) who was subsequently jailed for the theft.

Patrick Finucane's brother, Martin, stated that police roadblocks had been in place in close proximity to Patrick Finucane's home up to an hour before the murder; their removal prompted allegations that police had cleared the area so that the gunmen could have unfettered access to and from the house. Reports of police operations on that evening would be one documentary source to be examined by a wide-ranging independent inquiry into collusion, if it was initiated.

No one to date has been prosecuted for the murder and allegations of collusion by the security forces have yet to be the object of an independent inquiry. Amnesty International has monitored allegations about collusion because it was concerned in particular about allegations that members of the security forces used their official status to target Patrick Finucane for murder.

The killing of Patrick Finucane took place in the context of frequent allegations that police officers made regular threats against, or derogatory comments about, defence lawyers to detainees. Similar allegations continue to be made to this date.[11]

A year before Patrick Finucane's death in February 1989, Amnesty International had heard from a former detainee that, during interrogation at Castlereagh interrogation centre in Belfast, the police had branded Patrick Finucane as an accomplice of the IRA and said he should be killed:

"Detectives suggested that the UVF [another Loyalist paramilitary group] should shoot the solicitor. They further tried to discredit the solicitor saying that although the solicitors' hands were 'clean of guns' they should be shot as they are just as bad as the terrorists."

Patrick Finucane's wife said that the incidence of threats escalated during this time, both in terms of abuse directed against him to clients during interrogation and in terms of threatening telephone calls at his home. Five weeks before his death, one of his clients alleged that an RUC officer

"informed me that my solicitor was working for the IRA, and would meet his end .. He asked me to give Mr Finucane a message from him ... He told me to tell him he is a thug in a suit, a person trying to let on he is doing his job, and that he, like every other Fenian[12] bastard, would meet his end."

Loyalist sources also claimed that, prior to the killing, UDA members detained at Castlereagh had been told by detectives that Patrick Finucane and a few other solicitors "were helping to keep IRA gunmen out of prison". Although some of these Loyalists were later

31

arrested for other offences, apparently none of them had been questioned about these allegations.

However, Brian Nelson, the agent of British Military intelligence who also served as chief intelligence officer for the UDA, alleged <u>after</u> his conviction on other charges that he had directly assisted in the targeting of Patrick Finucane. According to a journal written by Brian Nelson while in prison, which was quoted in a television program[13], Brian Nelson was asked to gather information about Patrick Finucane some weeks prior to his killing, and he informed military intelligence officers of this request. Brian Nelson claimed that he passed a photograph to UDA operatives just a few days before the killing. Loyalist sources claimed that Brian Nelson pointed out Patrick Finucane's house to the gunmen. Brian Nelson was never charged in connection with the killing and his claims have never been examined in open court.

The widow of Patrick Finucane has issued a civil suit against the Ministry of Defence for damages for allegedly failing to pass on intelligence warnings that he was the target of Loyalist gunmen.

The killing of Patrick Finucane and the apparent lack of a thorough investigation into his killing has had wide ramifications for the public perception of the rule of law within Northern Ireland.

The Stevens Inquiry 1993

The Stevens inquiry in 1989-90, although ostensibly an inquiry into allegations of collusion, did not investigate the larger issues involved. The arrest and trial of Brian Nelson was another lost opportunity to examine in detail the role of official forces in shielding members of Loyalist armed groups that carry out killings of Republican suspects, if not in directly aiding and abetting in their actions.

According to press reports, the Stevens inquiry was reopened in the spring of 1993, after John Stevens was requested by the DPP, through the RUC Chief Constable, to head a further inquiry into matters outstanding after the trial of Brian Nelson. Press reports also indicated that the further inquiry was prompted by the revelations in Brian Nelson's prison journal, as well as allegations made in television programs about collusion. The only official statement about the inquiry, to be found in a press statement by Sir Hugh Annesley, the RUC Chief Constable[14], suggested that John Stevens' scope for action would be severely limited:

"The DPP asked me to pick up on one or two confidential issues which were part of the original inquiry and ask Stevens to give a personal view on them. I can categorically say there is no new inquiry. Stevens is not coming back to the province and has no men working here. I do not anticipate any other arrests or prosecutions."[15]

Notwithstanding the RUC's characterization of this initiative, Amnesty International believes that this inquiry must examine the crucial questions raised by Brian Nelson's revelations concerning the pro-active role of his military handlers. One of the key questions is whether the primary purpose of his recruitment was to gain intelligence on the UDA's activities in order to suppress it; or whether the primary purpose was to influence the UDA's targeting system away from the indiscriminate killing of Catholics towards IRA suspects. Linked to this question is the need to examine the reasons why the security forces did not take measures to stop the flow of intelligence files into the hands of Loyalist gunmen; and the role played by the security forces and services, including MI5, in heavily rearming Loyalist groups with South African weapons. In addition, other detailed questions should be investigated by John Stevens, including:

1. Did Brian Nelson's military handlers provide the UDA with photographs of suspects, as alleged?
2. Did the military handlers provide, as alleged, other crucial details about suspected targets, for example car registration numbers, addresses, movements, layouts of houses?
3. Did some handlers encourage a bombing campaign in the Republic of Ireland and an intimidation campaign of witnesses in an extortion trial, as alleged?
4. In how many instances of killings were warnings passed on by Brian Nelson? and in how many of these did military intelligence pass the information on to the RUC?
5. As an example of the above, were warnings passed on about the targeting of Patrick Finucane, and if not, why not?
6. Did other intelligence services have advance warning that Patrick Finucane was being targeted?

Finally, in view of the statement made by the British Army's General Officer Commanding, Lt-Gen Sir John Wilsey, in January 1993 that he was not ashamed of the army's role in the Nelson affair, the inquiry should reveal precisely what the army's role regarding Nelson and the UDA consisted of.

Other Allegations of Collusion

Amnesty International continues to receive regular reports that certain Catholics have been informed by the RUC that their names are on Loyalist "hit-lists". These people are not informed of any specific details which the Loyalists might have in addition to their names. Nor has it always been disclosed whether their names originated from security documents.[16] Members of the Catholic community continue to be killed by Loyalist gunmen in random attacks in Catholic areas, as well as in more selective killings of targeted individuals.

The group Relatives for Justice published a pamphlet[17] in July 1993 summarizing its concerns about alleged collusion and the denial to Catholics of equal protection under the law. They alleged that the RUC was negligent or incompetent in the gathering of evidence concerning Loyalist attacks on Catholics; that it failed to respond adequately to nationalist demands for protection; that it failed to deter Loyalist paramilitaries from entering Catholic areas or to detect them despite sophisticated surveillance; and that the RUC response to Loyalist attacks was slow and complacent and was not directed to the Loyalist areas to which gunmen escaped.

When killings by Loyalists take place it has sometimes been claimed that just before the killing there was a heavy security presence in the immediate area but that this was then removed, thus leading to the allegation that Loyalist gunmen were assured unfettered access to and from the scene of the crime. For this to occur, it would mean that the RUC would have had prior knowledge of such attacks to enable them to clear the area of a police presence at a critical moment; or that paramilitary gunmen had intimate knowledge of planned police movements as well as the timing of operational measures. The facility with which Loyalist gunmen raid homes in stringently monitored and controlled Catholic neighbourhoods and then leave without hindrance has contributed to the lack of confidence in the RUC to provide full protection for the Catholic community and to pursue Loyalists with the same vigour as the IRA is pursued.

Sinn Féin[18] member Alan Lundy was shot dead by UDA gunmen in May 1993 as he carried out repair work at the home of elected Sinn Féin Belfast city councillor Alex Maskey. The UDA later said it had intended to kill Alex Maskey. West Belfast Member of Parliament Dr Joe Hendron (SDLP)[19] accused the security forces of collusion, which was denied by the

RUC. He said "That loyalist gangsters can enter the heart of Andersonstown [a nationalist area in Belfast] on a busy Saturday evening firing shots with soldiers and police normally saturating the area, it does raise the question of collusion. I do believe this has happened and I do point the finger at the security forces" (Irish News, 3 May 1993). Sinn Féin spokespersons claimed there had been considerable security force activity - including regular identity checking, harassment and taking photographs of people working - around the home while the repair work was being carried out. It was claimed that on the day of the killing large armoured vehicles remained parked in the street for a number of hours, and then suddenly left.

Sinn Féin president Gerry Adams' wife and son were in their home when the UDA threw a grenade at it in June 1993. They were not injured. West Belfast SDLP councillor Alex Attwood said the attack raised serious questions about policing and the safety of nationalists in West Belfast. "Three times in recent months Loyalists have been able to strike with ease deep into West Belfast and attack the homes of Sinn Féin politicians and make their escape with equal ease. I am unable to move from my home off the Falls Road only yards from the scene of last night's attack without encountering or being stopped by the RUC or army. The very real perception among growing numbers of people is that there is collusion between the RUC and Loyalist paramilitaries, a perception that is fuelled by this latest attack and which is increasingly difficult to deny" (Irish News, 10 June 1993).

After an armed UDA gang opened fire in a betting shop in a Catholic area in April 1993, wounding five men, they drove away jeering and one of them shouted "You are all Fenian bastards". As they drove away the gunmen sprayed the area with more gunfire, injuring another man. Local people queried how such an attack could occur just 100 yards from an RUC station in Belfast. They also said that a security force patrol had just moved out of the area when the gunmen's car pulled up.

Further it is alleged that the security forces provide detailed layouts of suspects' homes to Loyalist gunmen. For example in the case of the killing of Patrick and Diarmuid Shields in January 1993 it was reported that several months before the shooting, the RUC had removed a legally-held shotgun without giving satisfactory reasons for this decision and had mapped out a layout of the family home. The gunmen shot two sons downstairs in their home, killing one and wounding another, before reportedly going straight to the bedroom where they shot the sleeping father. The family had run a shop which had been the subject of an intimidation campaign by Loyalist groups for several years, including a hoax bomb, sectarian slogan-painting on the walls and smashed windows.

There has recently been a great deal of controversy over the refusal of the RUC to issue firearms licences to individuals who have been threatened or even attacked. In addition there have been cases where people have had legally held guns taken away by the RUC without any explanation.

Eugene Martin was killed in February 1993 by two UVF gunmen who fired several times shooting him in the head at close range. A hunting rifle, legally held by Eugene Martin, had reportedly been removed by the RUC from his home prior to the attack. Catholic shop owner Patrick Shields also had his legally-held rifle reportedly removed (see above).

A North Belfast man was refused a permit for a firearm even though he had been warned by the RUC that his life was threatened by Loyalist paramilitaries, and even though his home had been attacked on two separate occasions. In April 1992 he applied for a firearm licence; in June RUC officers told him he was on a "hit list", and his home was attacked in December. He was refused the permit in January 1993, with no reasons given.

Sinn Féin councillor Gerard McGuigan was refused a firearms licence despite two Loyalist attacks on his home within 13 months. His house came under gun and grenade attack by the UDA/UFF in February 1992 and then a UDA/UFF bomb attack in March 1993 which narrowly missed injuring his wife and three children. He said, "My family is as entitled to protection as any other elected representative's family".

A Catholic shop owner believes he was the intended target for a UDA/UFF gun attack in his shop in April 1993. He arrived at the shop just after the attack. He claimed that there had been four patrols in the area at the time of the shooting, including an army foot patrol just 500 yards away. He had previously been told that documents with his personal details had gone missing from an army barracks and were in the hands of Loyalists. When he applied for permission to have a personal firearm he was refused. He also claimed that he had been harassed and threatened by security force patrols passing the shop; once they shouted, "What about you Kevin, it won't be long now."

SDLP spokespersons have claimed that the RUC is not even-handed in its dealings with both communities, when it comes to policing. West Belfast MP Dr Joe Hendron stated in September 1993, "[A]t times there does not seem to be the same will on behalf of the RUC to combat Loyalist terrorism. There is not the same level of security force presence in Loyalist areas. There is not the same number of police checkpoints in Loyalist areas." Father Denis Faul, a leading campaigner against both Republican and Loyalist violence, claimed that the security forces were negligent in protecting Catholic areas, after the killing of two Catholic council workers in October 1993. He claimed that after the Loyalist paramilitaries had issued threats of violence in retaliation for the Shankill Road IRA bombing of 23 October, the security forces should have provided checkpoints or security presence at all three main roads going into West Belfast. Father Faul has also commented on the difference in follow-up operations by the security forces following the killings of nationalists and those of their own members. It was reported, for example, that after the killing of the Patrick Shields, there was no follow-up search.

Following a failed UDA/UFF murder bid on a taxi driver in January 1993 in North Belfast, Dr Brian Feeney from SDLP said, "There is no way this should have occurred. It is beside Girdwood, one of the most heavily guarded army barracks in Belfast. The place is festooned with security equipment and cameras and almost certainly the guys who did this shooting were seen. But there was no follow-up operation in the area where these men were seen going into. People are asking why it is that the streets of the New Lodge and Ardoyne are flooded with soldiers on foot patrol but there is no comparable presence in the areas where Loyalists are coming from."

Another example is the killing of hairdresser Sean Hughes in West Belfast in September 1993. The Loyalist gunmen drove up the Falls Road (a predominantly Republican area) at one of the busiest times of the day and parked at the junction of one of the most frequently patrolled parts of West Belfast. After the killing a RUC officer admitted that this area was patrolled 24 hours per day, yet two men wearing baseball hats, dark glasses and gloves were able to walk through the area, enter the hairdressers shop and carry out their attack. The gunmen then walked back down the road and drove away. By this time local people had already informed the RUC of their car's description and registration number. It was alleged that no RUC checkpoints were established outside of West Belfast in order to catch the gunmen.

One explanation given for the heavier police/army presence in Republican areas is that the fear of ambush is much greater there than in Loyalist areas, where the security forces feel relatively safe. However, given that the RUC feel safer in Loyalist areas,[20] it is unclear why there should not be effective and immediate follow-up operations in such areas.

Others have alleged collusion between members of the security forces and Loyalist paramilitaries on the basis of their having been harassed and threatened by members of the security forces shortly before attacks. Sinn Féin election worker John Smith alleged that a June 1993 UVF attack on his home had been the culmination of being threatened and harassed by the security forces on numerous occasions. He said, "One time I had been stopped at a UDR checkpoint and my licence was removed. When it was returned there was an X between the eyes on the photograph, obviously a threat I was going to be shot." He had been told in August 1992 that intelligence files on him were in the hands of Loyalist paramilitaries.

The security forces in Northern Ireland have denied that there is any collusion between its members and Loyalist paramilitary groups, or that their approach to policing is not even-handed. An RUC spokesperson said in October 1993: "Police and soldiers have been working long hours in difficult and dangerous conditions to deal with terrorism from all quarters. To date this year [January to October], 189 Loyalists and 121 Republicans have been charged and large quantities of weapons and explosives have been found. This proves beyond doubt that there are no double standards on the part of the security forces, as has been suggested."[21]

Amnesty International's Concerns about Allegations of Collusion

For the last four years Amnesty International has been investigating serious allegations of collusion between members of the security forces and Loyalist armed groups. In the course of its work, Amnesty International has sought evidence to establish whether the government has done everything within its powers to investigate thoroughly allegations of collusion, and to wholly suppress collusion of the kind acknowledged in the Stevens inquiry. As part of this investigation the organization has sent delegates to the trial of Brian Nelson and the High Court hearing in the case against Channel Four television arising from a documentary program alleging widespread collusion (see below). Amnesty International has not been convinced that the government has taken adequate steps to halt collusion, to investigate thoroughly and make known the full truth about political killings of suspected government opponents, to bring to justice the perpetrators and dismantle "pro-state" organizations dedicated to political violence, or otherwise to deter such killings.

Allegations of collusion range from direct involvement of security force personnel in Loyalist "death squads"[22], complicity by authorities in such killings, to aiding and abetting such actions through the passing on of intelligence information.

Additionally, as noted, there are allegations that government authorities and the security forces do not have an even-handed approach to Republican and Loyalist armed groups. Government claims of even-handedness have been undermined by such factors as the characterization by high government and security officials of killings by Loyalists as strictly "reactive" to the violence of the Republican groups: a statement that could also apply to the use of force by the

security forces and so suggest a community of interest. The expression of such views suggests, rightly or
wrongly, that the security forces' view of Loyalist violence may be coloured by the fact that Loyalist groups
rarely, albeit with some exceptions, attack members
of the security forces. In fact, their victims are almost
entirely drawn from the Catholic community, except
when members of their own communities are subjected
to "punishment" beatings and shootings for alleged
criminal behaviour.

Whenever clandestine groups claim they are support-
ing a government's security forces and a governmen-
tal system through political killings, the governments
in question have a special obligation. Concrete measures are required to make absolutely clear they are
doing everything necessary to suppress such actions
and the groups behind them. In a situation of sectarian violence the importance of these obligations be-
comes more acute. This is the case in Northern Ireland where the victims of systematic killings and attacks by Loyalist groups are almost always members
of the minority Catholic community and often targeted
solely because of their religion. Amnesty International
condemns all such deliberate and arbitrary killings
and urges the government to take effective steps to
show incontrovertibly that it and its security forces
neither contribute to nor tolerate at any level unlawful killings by any of the parties to the violence in
Northern Ireland.

The revelations leading up to the establishment of the
Stevens inquiry should have been alarming enough
to any government to warrant a wide-ranging, independent (possibly judicial) inquiry into alleged collusion between members of the security forces and
armed Loyalist groups. Instead, government inaction
revealed an official reluctance to tackle head on, and
get to the bottom of, such serious allegations. The government did not institute any inquiry. The Chief Con-

stable of the RUC appointed John Stevens to lead a limited inquiry, the terms of reference being restricted to the immediate issue of missing security documents. This was a minimal response to a major crisis in public confidence: the inquiry did not investigate the overall pattern or the allegations that collusion had been going on for years. It did not examine evidence of anti-Catholic partiality and discriminatory treatment by security force personnel or the official response to incidents and allegations to this effect. Nor did the Stevens inquiry examine how the authorities — the police, the military, the security services as well as the prosecutorial service — had dealt with previous evidence of conspiracy to murder by members of armed Loyalist groups. Moreover, even though the most significant result of the Stevens inquiry was the arrest of Brian Nelson, the inquiry failed to investigate in depth the role of infiltrators and informers, or the level of knowledge attained by the security services of Loyalist paramilitary operations, let alone the specific allegations that intelligence agents helped Loyalist gunmen to target named Republican suspects.

The trial of UDA intelligence chief Brian Nelson revealed that a very high level of information on both Loyalist personnel and operations was held by the Army and the RUC. The trial also obliquely highlighted that little was done to disrupt these operations, to save lives, to dismantle Loyalist armed groups and to take severe measures to deter known collusion in the passing of security information. Brian Nelson's military handlers, who allegedly provided information which assisted in targeting some individuals for murder, were not charged with any offence.

Brian Nelson's trial and the claims of the Panorama television program were significant in another respect. They provided glimpses of the operations of Military Intelligence in relation to one agent in place. But it is widely acknowledged that Brian Nelson was not the only informer within the UDA, either for Military Intelligence or for the RUC or MI5. The question is posed whether information on the killings that did take place was known to the security forces through more than one agent and if so, why no action was taken to intercept the operations or to dismantle the organization once its leadership was identified as criminally involved in an ongoing conspiracy to murder. Amnesty International is deeply concerned about the implications arising out of these revelations for intelligence operations and the use of informers by all the security forces.

Amnesty International considers that a wide-ranging investigation is needed into the human rights implications of covert intelligence operations as well as into the specific allegations that through both action and deliberate inaction state authorities have been complicit in Loyalist murder operations.

The lack of determination, as shown in the trial of Brian Nelson, to investigate and reveal the full scope of his knowledge of his co-conspirators and the related evidence of collusion contrasts starkly with the determination with which the RUC pursued the Channel Four/Box Productions team over a <u>Dispatches</u> program on alleged collusion.[23] The vigour with which the RUC conducted its inquiry into the making of the program, including prolonged and repeated interrogation of those known to have been interviewed for the program, contrasted vividly with what is known of RUC investigative methods applied to Loyalist organizations and killings. During the Nelson trial the Crown expressed no interest in the identities and criminal responsibilities of other top members of the UDA. However, at the High Court hearing of contempt charges against Channel Four the Crown stressed that the identity of "Source A", withheld by the program makers, was crucial to any investigation of the allegations:

"quite apart from the fact that if there was any truth in the allegations made, `Source A' himself was involved in serious conspiracy to murder, as being a member of 'The Committee' in question, and was aware of others, and had information about others, who were themselves seriously involved in conspiracy to murder if not actual murder".

No comparable statement was made at the Brian Nelson trial concerning the leadership of the UDA, despite its characterization as a murderous organization, or the UDA's freedom to operate openly as such since it was founded in 1971[24].

The RUC response to the <u>Dispatches</u> program was to state emphatically that the allegations were wholly untrue. As stated in the RUC Chief Constable's statement immediately after the program,
"I utterly reject last night's program as an unjust and unsubstantiated slur on the good name of this Force ... [It] was long on accusation but lacking in usable or credible evidence" (<u>Independent</u>, 4 October 1991).

Similarly, the RUC did not establish (or encourage) an independent inquiry into the allegations made. The overall emphasis of the RUC was to discredit the program rather than to investigate fully the charges made. The overall thrust of the measures taken against the program makers, in turn, was to threaten and intimidate other investigative journalists who might contemplate reporting on evidence of collusion.

Even should particular allegations made in the <u>Dispatches</u> program not be borne out, an appropriate means to test their validity would have been an independent inquiry. In contrast, we saw a barrage of other measures: the unprecedented use of the Prevention of Terrorism Act to require disclosure of the identity of sources; the legal combination of contempt and perjury charges; the release - apparently by the RUC - of privileged information, provided by the program makers after the showing of the program, to selected newspapers; and the public disclosure of the names of those who were interviewed for the program, also apparently by the RUC. The latter action exposed these people to potential retaliation by the very "death squad" organizations alleged in the program to have had covert RUC support.

Amnesty International seeks in all situations to have human rights violations thoroughly investigated and the full truth made known. Thus the organization is concerned whenever measures are taken by governments which have the effect of obstructing or punishing efforts to investigate allegations of gross human rights abuse by government forces. The effect of the Channel Four/Box Productions prosecution and trial was to serve as a warning that the media could face major legal and financial challenges should journalists persist in seeking evidence of covert and unlawful government operations. The case has challenged journalists' ability to investigate covert action because it denied the right to withhold the identity of sources even if doing so would lead to human rights violations.

For the security forces to have the confidence of the public, they must be impartial and be seen to be impartial. For the government to have the confidence of the public, it has to be seen to ensure that its agents operate within the law and are accountable. For there to be accountability the government has to ensure openness and willingness to have its agents' actions scrutinized and, where necessary, that they are sanctioned for wrongdoing. However, for many years now, the government has been unwilling to have its agents' actions, as well as its own procedures, scrutinized by wide-ranging independent inquiries even though the pattern of violations called for such inquiries. The government has consistently refused to initiate such an inquiry into serious allegations that members of the security forces have on occasion operated a policy of deliberately killing alleged suspected members of armed groups rather than arresting them. The government has also refused to re-examine, through such an inquiry, both the legislation governing the use of lethal force and the existing procedures to investigate disputed killings and to make the full facts publicly known. Government practice on this issue is in violation of international standards. A similar reluctance to institute broad and independent inquiries into allegations of collusion with "death squads", that have been operating for over 20 years in the name of the political "status quo", has had dramatic consequences for public confidence.

As noted above, there is a particular need for openness to independent inquiries if the government is to show a real and effective commitment to the rule of law and to the suppression of violence. Amnesty International urges the government to establish a wide-ranging, thorough and impartial investigation into allegations of collusion between members of the security forces and armed Loyalist groups, as a measure that would signal the government's commitment to ensuring that its law enforcement agents operate within the rule of law.

Killings by Armed Political Groups

Introduction

Amnesty International opposes human rights abuses carried out by armed political groups, namely the torture or killing of prisoners, other deliberate and arbitrary killings and hostage-taking. In doing this, Amnesty International calls upon armed political groups to observe minimum humane standards, and cites norms of international humanitarian law (the laws of war) which apply certain minimum limitations on all parties to internal armed conflict. Above all international humanitarian law forbids governments and their opponents alike to torture any person, to deliberately kill civilians, to harm those who are wounded, captured or seeking to surrender, or to take hostages. These acts can never be justified. It also forbids the passing of sentences and carrying out of executions without a previous judgment by a recognized court and without due process of law. Amnesty International, of course, opposes executions without qualification, under any circumstances.

In opposing abuses by armed political groups Amnesty International neither recognizes nor extends any particular status to such groups; its concerns are with the victims and the potential victims. Nor does the organization's intervention imply that a conflict has attained a particular threshold of intensity: Amnesty International aims to promote observance of minimum humane standards as widely as possible and wherever political groups turn to violence.

In the United Kingdom Amnesty International opposes the practices of both Loyalist and Republican groups of taking or holding people hostage, of torture or ill-treatment (whether systematic beatings or acts, such as "knee-capping", resulting in permanent maiming), or in threatening with death or deliberately killing civilians, captives or those who have been incapacitated.

Human Rights Abuses by Republican Armed Groups

The dominant Republican armed group is the Irish Republican Army (IRA). Its members come mainly from the Catholic minority in Northern Ireland. The IRA's stated aims are to fight for the unification of Northern Ireland with the Republic of Ireland, and for a withdrawal of British army forces from Northern Ireland. Violence in the form of bombings is directed primarily at economic and business centres of Northern Ireland and in the form of bombings and shootings directed at members of the security forces. Civilians have been frequently killed as a result of such operations. The IRA also carries out killings of alleged members of Loyalist armed groups, of alleged informers, and of civilians who it believes in any way assist in maintaining the presence of security forces in Northern Ireland. In addition, the IRA carries out so-called "punishment" shootings and beatings of members of the Catholic community who are described as participating in "anti-social activities".

IRA Bombings and Killings in Northern Ireland

In 1990 the IRA claimed responsibility for 44 killings, in 1991 for 40 killings and in 1992 for 29 killings in Northern Ireland. Hundreds of civilians were injured and many permanently maimed in IRA attacks in which the safety of civilians was utterly disregarded.

Members of the security forces have been a key target for Republican armed groups. In 1991, 16 of the 40 people killed by the IRA were members of the security forces; in 1992 nine of 29 people killed by the IRA were members of the security forces.

A policewoman, Colleen McMurray, died and another RUC officer lost both legs in an IRA bomb attack on their patrol car in Newry, County (Co.) Down, in March 1992. A 2,000 pound bomb exploded behind an army border checkpoint at Newry in May 1992, killing one soldier and wounding two soldiers, two RUC officers and a passing woman motorist. An off-duty RUC officer, Jim Douglas, was shot dead in October 1992 as he was drinking in a bar in the centre of Belfast. The first member of the Royal Irish Regiment (RIR) to be killed since its formation in July 1992 was ambushed and shot dead in Co. Antrim in October 1992. Off-duty RIR soldier Ian Warnock was shot dead in front of his three-year-old son while waiting to collect his wife from work in November 1992. He was sitting in his car when the gunmen's taxi pulled up alongside and he was fired on from close range with an automatic weapon. His son was not hurt. Another off-duty RIR soldier, Stephen Waller, was on leave from garrison duty in Cyprus when he was shot dead at his home in Belfast in December 1992. Off-duty part-time RUC officer, Reggie Williamson, was killed by a car bomb near Armagh. His girlfriend, who was driving behind him, witnessed the explosion. Off-duty RIR soldier, Christopher Wren, was killed in June 1993 when a bomb exploded beneath his car in Co. Derry.

RUC officer Michael Ferguson had been dealing with a shoplifting case in a crowded shopping street in Londonderry in January 1993 when a lone gunman approached him and shot him twice in the head. In February 1993 one soldier was killed and four others wounded by an elaborate boobytrap in Armagh. An initial explosion hit a joint RUC/army patrol, injuring at least one soldier. It was followed by two simultaneous explosions designed to injure or kill soldiers going to the aid of the first bomb's casualties.

A number of policemen and soldiers have been shot dead in sniping attacks. Newspaper reports stated that the IRA had sniper rifles which were accurate at up to a mile. Soldier Damien Shackleton was hit by a number of rounds while patrolling a Belfast area in August 1992. The IRA had held a family hostage in their home and used it to ambush the patrol. Another soldier was shot in the same month near Crossmaglen while on patrol. In November 1992 RUC officer Alan Corbett was shot at a joint police-army checkpoint in Co. Fermanagh. In February 1993 RUC officer John Reid was shot while accompanying an army patrol in fields near Crossmaglen. In March, June and July 1993 three soldiers were shot in South Armagh. In November RUC reservist, Brian Woods, was shot while at a checkpoint in Newry.

In blatant violation of international humanitarian standards, the IRA bombed the Musgrave Park Hospital in Belfast in November 1991, killing two soldiers and injuring ten people. Among the wounded were four military personnel and a girl aged five. The dead and injured were watching a rugby match on television in the staff social club when the bomb exploded.

Ellen Sefton, wife of a former RUC officer, was killed along with him in a bomb attack in June 1990. The couple were driving in their car when a boobytrap bomb exploded under their car; the car then went out of control, injuring two elderly people.

A Catholic nun, Sister Catherine Dunne, was killed by a landmine along with three RUC officers in July 1990 near Armagh. Sister Catherine was driving towards Armagh when her car was caught in the explosion and tossed into a hedge; her companion, a social worker, was seriously injured. The unmarked police car was thrown 80 feet over a ditch and all but disintegrated.

In the last two years the town centres of Dungannon, Lurgan, Craigavon, Londonderry, Magharafelt, Bangor, Lisnaskea, Newry, Newtownards, Strabane, Belfast and many others have been bombed causing millions of pounds' worth of damage.[25] Many bombing attacks have also resulted in injuries to civilians. The September 1992 bombing of the government Forensic Laboratories in Belfast caused damage to 700 homes in a predominantly Protestant area, two hospitals and some churches; 23 people were treated in hospital for minor injuries.

In September 1992 David Dougan, a Presbyterian church caretaker and father of four, was critically wounded after being shot through the kitchen window. The IRA claimed he was a member of the RIR but this was denied. His death provoked comments about the vulnerability of the Protestant community in border areas.

In August 1992 Isobel Leyland was shot dead by an IRA sniper who had apparently been aiming at a joint army/police patrol. Isobel Leyland had left Northern Ireland after her younger brother was killed by Loyalists in 1975 and had returned there briefly to visit her elderly mother when she was killed. In June 1992, 21 people were injured in an explosion when an IRA man leapt from a crowd in a busy shopping area in Belfast and placed a limpet mine on the roof of a police car. Two police officers and 19 civilians were injured.

The killing of civilians providing services to the security forces is in breach of minimum humane standards. Between 1985 and September 1993 the IRA killed 30 people for doing contract work for the security forces. Hundreds more have been forced to give up work after being threatened and scores of businesses have been intimidated into halting supplies. The targets have included: timber merchants, fruit and vegetable suppliers, cement firms and civil engineers. In January 1992 eight Protestant workers were killed and five injured when a building company's minibus, in which they were travelling, was blown up in an explosion near Teebane Crossroads in Co. Tyrone. They were on the way home from working on a British Army base. In September 1993 Adrian McGovern, a father of four, was gunned down on the doorstep of his home while looking after his children. His killers held a close friend hostage, took his lorry and drove it right up to the house luring Adrian McGovern out to greet his supposed friend. The IRA claimed he had been supplying the security forces with building materials.

The IRA carried out bombings using so-called "human bombs". In October 1990 Patsy Gillespie, a civilian who worked in an army kitchen, was abducted and forced, through threats to his family, to drive a bomb to a checkpoint where it exploded, killing him and five soldiers. In the meantime, his wife was held hostage by masked men and was assured that he would return to her unharmed. In April 1991 a woman, who worked as a domestic cleaner at a police station, was forced to carry a bomb in her handbag through the village to the police station while her husband and child were held hostage. Nobody was hurt when the bomb exploded.

In October 1993 the IRA bombed a fish shop in the Shankill Road, a predominantly Protestant area, when the shop and street were crowded with civilians. An IRA statement said that the target was a meeting of members of the UDA/UFF in a room above the shop. The bomb resulted in the death of nine Protestant civilians, including seven-year-old Michelle Baird with her parents and 13-year-old Leanne Murray, and in the death of the IRA man who had placed the bomb. In addition over 50 people were injured; no alleged members of the UDA/UFF were among the dead.

"Punishment" Shootings and Beatings

The following statistics on torture and maimings through "punishment" beatings and shootings are based on police figures. These figures would necessarily have to be taken as minimum figures, as victims of such treatment would not always require hospitalization and therefore would not always be recorded, and because those that do require hospitalization do not always divulge the reason for the injuries. In 1991 there were 36 reported punishment shootings and 40 punishment beatings by Republican armed groups. In 1992 there were 59 punishment shootings. The main age group affected by such "punishments" is under 30, and on the whole the victims are male.

In December 1991 Amnesty International was informed that the IRA was reviewing its policy of "knee-capping" with a view to stopping its usage. However, subsequently "punishment" shootings, including "knee-capping", have continued, sometimes resulting in the amputation of limbs and in one instance in death. In December 1992 John Collett was shot in the legs in his house; both legs were amputated and he later died from his injuries. On New Year's Day in 1993 Christopher Donnelly, aged 22, from Dungannon, was shot in both legs by the IRA in front of his mother. One of his legs was subsequently amputated and he was ordered to leave Northern Ireland upon release from hospital. Micky Sherlock, aged 20, also had a leg amputated after being "kneecapped" in August 1992. He was told to leave but the "expulsion order" was lifted after the amputation. They were shot for alleged "anti-social" behaviour. Tommy Smith and Phil McCullough were shot in the legs for alleged "joy-riding" (driving around in a stolen car); Phil McCullough developed gangrene.

Damien McCartan, aged 21, was shot three times in the legs in March 1993 after refusing to allow his car to be used by IRA men in an attack. The IRA issued a statement that he had been shot as "punishment" for endangering the lives of "IRA volunteers" and risking the capture of "war materials". In the same month Edward Kane, aged 27, was knee-capped in both knees and shot in both elbows; as a result he will be permanently maimed, with one arm being totally immobile and a limp in one leg. Before his hospital treatment had been fully completed he was forced under threat of death to leave Northern Ireland.

Danny Morris, aged 18, was taken to hospital in January 1992 and treated for a broken leg, broken arm and serious wounds to the other leg. His mother claimed that a gang of eight men held him down and beat him and tried to hammer a chisel into his leg in three places. He was ordered by the IRA to leave Northern Ireland within 48 hours of his release from hospital.

Three teenagers, Peter Burns, 18, Patrick Daly, 19, and Stephen Mallon, aged 17, were beaten by seven masked men armed with baseball bats and iron bars in April 1992. The three were tied around the feet, their hands bound behind their backs and then were beaten on the ankles, knees and elbows. They sustained broken limbs and severe bruising.

In dozens of cases annually the IRA ordered people to leave Northern Ireland under threat of being physically assaulted if the order was not carried out. In 1991 David Madigan and Liam Cairns were driven out of Newry at risk of their lives; they spent about ten months in hiding in Northern Ireland before being allowed to return to their homes. In September 1992 Desmond Havern was ordered to leave the Newry area immediately. In January 1993 the IRA ordered six people out of Londonderry and another person out of Co. Tyrone. The IRA claimed that it had tied up

two of the youths and doused them with paint, allegedly for engaging in criminal activities.

Alleged informers are a key target for torture and
murder by the IRA. During 1992 at least six people
were killed for allegedly informing to the security
forces. In July the IRA shot dead three IRA members,
Gregory Burns, Aidan Starrs and John Dignam, claiming that the three had been involved in murdering
Margaret Perry a year earlier to prevent her from
exposing their involvement in a robbery. The IRA also
claimed that Starrs and Dignam had admitted to their
roles in the murder to the RUC and had been given
immunity from prosecution in exchange for them be-
coming informers. Brendan McWilliams was shot dead
in April, Robin Hill was seized and shot dead in August, and Gerard Holmes in November. During 1993
the IRA killed Christopher Harte in February, and
Joseph Mulhern in June. The families of some of these
victims disputed the allegations.

The IRA's rules setting out disciplinary procedures
are to be found in a handbook known as "The Green
Book". An alleged informer would be subjected to an
IRA court martial which allegedly consists of the following: the accused is abducted, taken to a hiding place
and interrogated, usually while held blindfolded or
hooded; once a confession has been extracted, the accused is then brought before a secret court martial,
usually presided over by a senior IRA figure, who
passes sentence. Under the Orders, there is a mandatory death penalty for certain breaches, including
"treason" and "treachery".[26]

IRA actions in Britain

The main actions by the IRA in England in the 1990s have
been bombing attacks on shopping centres, railway
stations and more recently the financial centre, known
as the City of London. The IRA has claimed that dur-

ing 1992 it carried out 46 bomb attacks and on 1,060 occasions its actions made commuter traffic and businesses grind to a halt. In 1992 four civilians were killed as a result of IRA attacks in England, and by November 1993, three civilians had been killed.

Both the massive bombs in the City of London led to deaths of civilians. In April 1992 an IRA bomb in the City resulted in three deaths and in over 90 injuries; the civilians killed included 15-year-old Daniella Carter. In April 1993 a huge explosion in the City killed Edward Henty, a journalist, and injured more than 40 people.

In February 1993 bomb attacks were carried out at a gas works in Warrington and then 48 hours later in a crowded north London shopping area injuring 18 people. In March two bombs exploded at mid-day on a Saturday in a busy shopping centre in Warrington killing two children: Johnathan Ball, aged 3, and Tim Parry, aged 12, and injuring over 50 people. When the first bomb went off, Tim Parry had run for shelter directly into the blast of the second bomb. After this bombing and the high level of public condemnation, the IRA announced that it would abandon bomb attacks in public areas, where there is a high risk of civilian casualties, and would concentrate instead on political and military targets.[27] However, in September and October there were over ten bombing attacks in shopping areas throughout North London; no one was injured as a result of these attacks.

IPLO and INLA Killings

Other Republican armed groups, although smaller in membership and power, have engaged in similar actions. The Irish People's Liberation Organization (IPLO) disbanded in November 1992 after reportedly being put under considerable pressure by the IRA to do so, on the grounds that some of its members had engaged in drug dealing. The IPLO had killed five people during 1992, including some in sectarian attacks on Protestants. In May 1992 a gunman opened fire at random in a bar in a Loyalist area, killing a pensioner and wounding two men. The IPLO statement claimed that it "would not stand by and allow sectarian slaughter of innocent nationalists without exacting similar retribution".

Another organization, the Irish National Liberation Army (INLA), was reportedly reactivated in 1992 and carried out a number of murders and attempted murders. INLA gunmen wounded Darren Quigley in August 1992 after hitting him with three shotgun blasts at close range. In January 1993 they killed Samuel Rock whose alleged links with the (Loyalist) UDA were forcefully denied by relatives.

Human Rights Abuses by Loyalist Armed Groups

The main Loyalist armed groups are the Ulster Defence Association (UDA) (which also acts under the name of the Ulster Freedom Fighters, the UFF) and the Ulster Volunteer Force (UVF). They draw their membership from the Protestant community and are known as Loyalists because they favour Northern Ireland remaining a part of the United Kingdom. The stated aim of their operations is to counter the Republican threat to the continued existence of Northern Ireland as part of the UK and this is done in part through acts of intimidation and violence in Catholic areas. To this end, their activities include bombings and killings of suspected members of Republican armed groups as well as random attacks on ordinary Catholics. The UDA was banned in August 1992 in Northern Ireland, but not in Britain where it is alleged that about one-tenth of its income is raised.

It has become increasingly clear that firearms used in Loyalist killings - which have been claimed by different Loyalist organizations - come from a common "arms pool". Press reports have suggested that this "arms pool" may be organized by Ulster Resistance, a group formed in the mid-1980s in opposition to the Anglo-Irish Agreement but now largely inactive. This group is reportedly still in possession of its share of a haul of South African arms imported in the 1980s (see page 20). The main Loyalist organizations have reportedly drawn on this "pool" not only for weapons but also for intelligence. They carry out operations not only in their own names but also under names like the Red Hand Commandos, Red Branch Knights and the Loyalist Retaliation Action Group. In 1992 the UDA and the UVF formed a Combined Loyalist Military Command, which occasionally meets to discuss strategy.

Killings by Loyalist Armed Groups

Since 1990 the number of killings by Loyalist groups has sharply increased. They claimed responsibility for 19 killings in 1990, 41 killings in 1991 and 34 killings in 1992.

The main victims of Loyalist killings are ordinary members of the Catholic community. Out of the 34 people killed in 1992, only five were known Republicans or were reported to have been involved in paramilitary activity.

Peter Fegan, a Catholic, travelled from the Republic of Ireland to Belfast for the first time in October 1991, where he visited a number of pubs (bars), mainly in a Protestant area. In one pub he was grabbed by four youths who dragged him into the basement of a block of flats where he was beaten and shot in the mouth, arm and back of the head; he lay there for 17 hours before being found. The UDA/UFF issued a statement saying it had "executed" an "IRA spy"; this claim was dismissed by the police who said that the motive was sectarian.

Terry McConville, Catholic father of three, was killed in March 1992 by the UVF in Portadown. In the middle of the night, a gunman used a crowbar to force open the front door, ran upstairs first into the daughter's bedroom, then into another bedroom where the victim was shot. His wife, a Protestant, chased the killer along the street where many houses have been abandoned and boarded up.

In January 1993 Sharon McKenna, a Catholic, was visiting a Protestant friend who had just returned from hospital. She was cooking a meal when UVF gunmen arrived at the door and shot her twice, once in the back and then in the head.

Random attacks are justified as attacks on the "Republican community" which means on people living in an area broadly deemed to be nationalist.

Five people were shot dead and seven injured when UDA/UFF gunmen opened random fire at short range into a crowded betting shop with a largely Catholic clientele in south Belfast in February 1992. A total of 47 shots were fired, hitting everyone in front of the customers' counter. Among those killed were 15-year-old James Kennedy and 18-year-old Peter Magee.

The UDA/UFF opened fire using a submachine gun on another betting office in north Belfast in November 1992. After firing they lobbed a grenade among the injured and dead. Three people were killed and 12 injured (among the injured were at least two Protestants). A further attack by the UFF on a betting shop in Belfast failed in December 1992 when the gun jammed.

Three men were injured, two of them seriously, after UDA/UFF gunmen opened fire through the doors of a mainly Catholic dockers' club in Belfast in September 1992. This took place during a charity function, attended by both Protestants and Catholics, in aid of a hospice.

Craigavon teenagers Eileen Duffy and Catriona Rennie were shot dead by the UVF in March 1991 while working at the counter of a van serving as a mobile shop. A man who tried to assist them was also killed.

UVF gunmen opened fire on a pub in a Catholic village in Co. Down in November 1992, killing one man and injuring three others.

Seven people, including at least one Protestant, were killed in October 1993 and 11 people injured when UDA/UFF gunmen sprayed a packed pub with automatic gunfire. The attack took place in the seaside village of Greysteel, eight miles from Londonderry. The UFF said in a statement: "This is the continuation of our threat against the nationalist electorate that they would pay a heavy price for last Saturday's slaughter of nine Protestants". (This was a reference to the IRA bombing of a fish shop in the Shankill Road the previous week.)

Random firing into houses by Loyalist gunmen is a common occurrence. In September 1992 a teenage Catholic girl was shot and injured shielding her week-old baby brother after gunmen fired through a living room window, having failed to break down the door of the house in north Belfast. They then attacked the house next door, wounding a man. In October, again in north Belfast, six shots were fired through a living room window, missing a father and his six-year-old son, and hitting the cot of a five-day-old baby who was uninjured. In January 1993 two people were shot randomly on a street in north Belfast, one Protestant and one Catholic. In February 1993, Tommy Molloy was shot dead in Co. Armagh when UVF gunmen fired into the home while he was watching television with three children; one child was slightly injured.

Members of Sinn Féin and their relatives have been targeted for killing. Sinn Féin advice centres have also been attacked with random gunfire attacks and bombings. Election workers for Sinn Féin have also been under attack.

In April 1992 Danny Cassidy was shot dead by the UDA/UFF. He had canvassed for a Sinn Féin candidate during the general election. His wife claimed that in the seven days prior to his death, he had twice been stopped by the police and threatened that he would be killed. A local Social Democratic and Labour Party (SDLP) councillor made an official complaint, based on eyewitness accounts, about this harassment. Eyewitnesses told him that in the first incident the police had thrown Danny Cassidy against a van and pointed a rifle to his head. In the second incident, a priest saw Cassidy being spreadeagled by the police in the town centre, one of whom pointed a gun at his chest while two others searched his pockets. After his death the RUC initially denied that a complaint had been made; once it became clear that a complaint had been lodged a senior officer was appointed to investigate the harassment. Dr Edward Daly, the Bishop of Londonderry, said there was clear evidence that Danny Cassidy had suffered "constant, cruel and public harassment and humiliation from some units of the police" and that given the sectarian murders "it is unjust, irresponsible and wrong for police officers to pick out and highlight individuals in this public manner, thus putting their lives in mortal danger".

In October 1992 law student Sheena Campbell, mother of a 10-year-old son and a former Sinn Féin parliamentary candidate, was shot dead by UVF gunmen in a hotel bar in the university area of Belfast. In December 1992 Malachy Carey, a former Sinn Féin candidate, was shot dead by the UDA/UFF.

Philomena Hanna, aged 26 and mother of two, was killed after being shot five times in the face and body by the UDA/UFF in April 1992. She worked in a chemist shop, providing a service of delivering oxygen cylinders to both communities. The UDA/UFF wrongly claimed that she had a brother in Sinn Féin. The gun used to kill Philomena Hanna had previously been used also in killings attributed to the Red Hand Commandos.

In September 1992 the UVF killed an elderly couple, Charles and Teresa Fox, in Co. Tyrone because of claims that some family members had Republican connections. The Fox's son-in-law and his uncle had also been killed by the UVF nine months earlier.

In August 1993 Sean Lavery, the son of Sinn Féin councillor Bobby Lavery, was killed after UDA/UFF gunmen fired into the living room of the house and shot him as he watched television in the sitting room. Sinn Féin councillors protested in early August that they had all been denied financial assistance to install bullet-proof windows, something which was not denied to SDLP councillors under threat. Such a bullet-proof window would have saved the life of Sean Lavery. Similarly, a number of leading members of the SDLP carry firearms, but no Sinn Féin members at that time had been granted firearms certificates by the RUC. Mark Durkan, the chairperson of the SDLP, said: "Refusing certain people weapons insinuates that violence against them is acceptable while violence against other politicians is not."

A Sinn Féin election worker, John Smith, escaped injury in a UVF attack in June 1993. He was at home with his wife and two children when two gunmen attempted to smash into the house with a sledgehammer. When that failed, they fired four shots through the bedroom window. He said that the RUC had warned him that he was being targeted by Loyalist paramilitaries.

Loyalists have claimed that attacks on constitutional nationalists and groups, like the Gaelic Athletic Association (GAA) which espoused Irish nationalism were legitimate targets because they were seen by Loyalists to be behind the "cutting edge" of IRA violence. This was stated by the UDA in January 1993; the statement also labelled the SDLP as part of a "pannationalist front", consisting of the IRA, Sinn Féin, the SDLP and the Irish Government. In August 1993 the Red Hand Commandos warned that Irish traditional music was part of the "pan-nationalist front" and warned that it would bomb bars and hotels which held folk music nights (including in the Republic of Ireland).

In January 1993 the UVF shot dead 51-year-old Patrick Shields and his 20-year-old son, Diarmuid, in Co. Tyrone. The gunmen killed the son downstairs in the house, seriously wounded another son who tried to barricade the door, and then shot the father who lay in bed. Patrick Shields was prominent in the organization of the local GAA. In the same month the UVF issued a warning to the West Belfast Soccer League, saying "Don't you fenian b... come up the Ormeau Park again." The threat affected 12 teams from all over the city who include both Protestant and Catholic members. The League was forced to cancel its weekly games in Ormeau Park. In February arsonists attacked a GAA club in north Belfast; it was the twelfth attack on the football club since the early 1970s.

During 1993 there were around 15 attacks on homes of prominent SDLP members. They began with incendiary attacks carried out on the homes of two SDLP councillors in Belfast in February 1993. The UDA claimed responsibility and stated "This is a small reminder that their party's 'brothers in arms' stance with Sinn Féin has not gone unnoticed." In July the UDA/UFF launched coordinated bomb attacks at the homes of three prominent members of the SDLP; no one was hurt. At the same time a gunman fired 13 times through the window of SDLP councillor Annie Armstrong's house, hitting the television and narrowly missing the family.

Another group which has been targeted is taxi drivers; many taxi firms are identified with either the Catholic or the Protestant communities. During 1991 six taxi drivers were killed by Loyalists, five Catholics and one Protestant. In February 1992 Paddy Clarke, an executive member of the Conradh na Gaeilge (Gaelic League) was shot by the UDA/UFF while watching television with his wife and six-year-old son. He was the seventh employee of the West Belfast Taxi Association to be killed by Loyalists since the early 1970s. In March 1992 the UDA/UFF wounded a Catholic taxi driver, shot six times while he was waiting to pick up a child for school. He was an Irish-language activist and governor of an Irish school. In June the UDA/UFF wounded another taxi driver as he waited to pick up a fare in Belfast. Hours earlier another taxi driver in Bangor was attacked as shots were fired into his home.

In October 1992 the UVF placed a bomb outside the Belfast offices of the newspaper Sunday World. The UVF statement said: "We will not stand by while the poison pen does its best to vilify our volunteers". Specific death threats were also issued against two journalists working on the newspaper.

Although it has not been part of the strategy of Loyalist armed groups to attack the security forces, recently the Loyalist community has been reacting to a perceived tougher stance by the RUC within the Protestant areas. In February on two separate occasions shots were fired at the RUC; there have been violent incidents in the Shankill Road area; and there have also been Loyalist attacks on prison officers, including the killing of Protestant prison officer Jim Peacock in September 1993. In June 1993 UVF member Brian McCallum was killed by his own grenade, allegedly intended for use against the RUC, at an Orange Order parade which had been rerouted away from Catholic areas. The riots that accompanied his funeral at the beginning of July were described by the police as the worst civil unrest within the Protestant community seen since the signing of the Anglo-Irish Agreement. There were 35 shootings, 11 bomb attacks and 63 hijackings over one weekend. The UDA and the UVF claimed that the violence was a result of the increased harassment by the RUC over the previous three months.

"Punishment" Shootings and Beatings

The following statistics on punishment beatings and shootings by armed groups are based on police figures. As noted with regard to statistics on IRA abuses, these figures have to be taken as minimum figures. In 1991, 40 punishment shootings and 22 punishment beatings were carried out by Loyalist armed groups. In 1992 there were 74 punishment shootings by Loyalists. The main age group affected by these "punishments" is under 30, and on the whole the victims are male.

During 1992 four Protestants were killed by Loyalist groups for being alleged informers. David Boyd was shot dead in January by the UDA/UFF; Peter Clements was shot dead in April by the UVF; Edward

McCreery was shot dead in April by the UDA/UFF; and Michael Anderson was shot dead in October by the Red Hand Commandos.

In November 1992 Donna Wilson was brutally beaten to death by a gang of up to ten men wielding baseball bats and pickaxe handles. One of three men also beaten by the gang was hospitalized with two broken legs. Her neighbours had previously petitioned the authorities to have her evicted because of noisy parties in her flat.

Interviews by a journalist with eight kneecapped youths pointed to an alienated subculture in which "hoods" were pitted against gunmen in a sort of gang warfare that had nothing to do with politics or religion. "In my crowd, it was either crime or paramilitary groups. I chose crime", said Robert Hutchinson, a 19-year-old Protestant who had been badly beaten several times. He and others said they get a "buzz" from bucking authority - whether it's the police or the paramilitaries. "They both think they're God, telling you what to do," said Ian Sanlon, a kneecapped joyrider.[28]

According to the group Families Against Intimidation and Terror, the Ulster Young Militants (UYM) have been used to carry out punishment attacks on other teenagers within their own areas. The UYM issued a warning in September 1993 that "no warning" attacks would follow on suspected drug dealers. A spokesperson said: "We are connected to the UDA and take our policy from the UDA. We see ourselves as policing our own areas and are better equipped to deal with the drug problem in particular, given the age of our members." In December 1991 a UYM member, Stephen Willis, was jailed for ten years after accidentally killing his friend and fellow member Stephen Audley with a gun provided by the UDA. The two had apparently been given the gun to carry out a "knee-capping" on a suspected robber. A third UYM member, Brian McCall, was jailed for his role in the aborted knee-capping attempt.

Amnesty International's Concerns and Action

Amnesty International opposes hostage taking; torture or ill-treatment (whether systematic beatings or violent acts, such as "knee-capping", resulting in permanent maiming); or threatening with death or deliberately killing civilians, captives or those who have been incapacitated. It does so irrespective of whether the perpetrators are Republican or Loyalist.

In recent years Amnesty International has condemned human rights abuses in initiatives on a number of cases in Northern Ireland. In July 1992 Amnesty International condemned the killings of three people, Gregory Burns, Aidan Starrs and John Dignam by the IRA, which alleged that the three had been police informers. In a public statement Amnesty International drew parallels to three killings carried out by Protestant armed organizations which Amnesty International equally condemned. These included the shooting in 1992 of David Boyd by the UDA/UFF, who alleged he was a police informer; the killing by the UVF of one of its own members, Peter Clements, because of alleged "treason"; and the killing by the UDA/UFF of Edward McCreery on allegations that he had been found "guilty of collusion" with the police.

In April of this year Amnesty International published a news item in which it called on all Republican and Loyalist armed groups to halt torture, maiming and killing of civilians. This was in response to an incident in which a young Catholic man, Damian McCartan, had been shot three times in the legs by the IRA for refusing to allow his car to be used by the IRA.

In June the organization expressed its concern about the case of Edward Kane who was shot in both knees and both elbows as a "punishment" in March 1993 in Northern Ireland by the IRA. Amnesty International condemned the action taken against Mr. Kane and called for the death threat against him to be rescinded.

Amnesty International again made a public appeal for an end to deliberate and arbitrary killings by all parties to the civil conflict in Northern Ireland after a week in October 1993 in which 23 people were killed and many others injured. The killings were carried out by both Republican and Loyalist armed groups.

Amnesty International continues to urge the leadership of armed political groups to take steps to ensure that their members:

* don't torture
* don't kill prisoners
* don't kill civilians
* don't take hostages

Footnotes

1 Mark Urban, <u>Big Boys' Rules</u> (Faber and Faber, London, 1992).

2 The Criminal Law Revision Committee recommended that the charge of manslaughter should be brought for the use of excessive force in self-defence or in the prevention of crime. See also, "Legal Controls on the use of Lethal Force: Options for Reform", by Professor Tom Hadden, March 1993, published in the <u>Eighteenth Report of the Standing Advisory Commission on Human Rights</u>.

3 See <u>Killings by Security Forces in Northern Ireland</u>, June 1988; <u>Investigating Lethal Shootings: The Gibraltar Inquest</u>, April 1989; and <u>Human Rights Concerns</u>, June 1991. See also a pamphlet produced by the Committee on the Administration of Justice entitled <u>Inquests and Disputed Killings in Northern Ireland</u>, January 1992.

4 The title of the Special Rapporteur was changed in 1993 to the Special Rapporteur on extrajudicial, summary or arbitrary executions.

5 The European Commission on Human Rights has recently considered two cases in relation to the use of lethal force in Northern Ireland.
    In <u>Kelly v UK</u>, the driver of a stolen car was shot by soldiers while apparently trying to escape from soldiers at a checkpoint, and in the process hitting several vehicles and injuring two soldiers. As the car drove away, soldiers fired 14-15 rounds, killing the driver and injuring two other passengers. The High Court judge, during a claim for compensation, found that the soldiers had a reasonable belief that the occupants of the car were terrorists making a determined attempt to escape and that the soldiers shot at the car in order to prevent further crimes and to effect arrest. Kelly's father argued, in his application to the European Commission, that the killing could not be regarded as "absolutely necessary" and was disproportionate. The Commission decided in 1993 that the case was inadmissible and concluded that in the circumstances the use of lethal force had been justified.
    In <u>McCann, Farrell & Savage v UK</u>, the European Commission decided in September 1993 that the application concerning the killing of three IRA members by the SAS in Gibraltar in 1988 was admissible. The Government submitted that the European Commission should not look beyond the inquest findings of lawful killing, implicit in which was a rejection of any plot to kill the three deceased, and an acceptance that the degree of force used was proportionate to the aim of protecting life. The applicants submitted that the vagueness of UK law on the use of force (lack of clear, detailed rules strictly limiting and controlling the use of lethal force), together with the training on the use of firearms, the particular briefing given to the SAS soldiers, the factual context surrounding the killings, and the inadequacy of

the subsequent police investigation and inquest resulted in a violation of Article 2 of the European Convention on Human Rights.

6 In May 1989 two members of the security forces had been given 18-month suspended sentences for possessing documents containing information which was likely to be useful to [Loyalist] terrorists (including the photographs, names and addresses of suspects). One of them remained in the British Army. Because they pleaded guilty, their trial was brief - the Crown did not go into detail about what the two had said during interrogation (that is, that they passed on these documents knowing or suspecting that they could be used for murder). They were not charged with conspiracy to murder; nor were any of the named Loyalists who received the documents. However, Terence McDaid, the brother of one of the persons on one of the photo-montages in question, was killed at the address provided, apparently mistakenly.

7 Brian Nelson was arrested in early 1990 and his trial took place in January 1992.

8 BBC Panorama program "The Dirty War", broadcast in June 1992.

9 Panorama program, June 1992.

10 British intelligence services alleged a breakdown of their own intelligence and surveillance operations. However, Brian Nelson claimed that he was told that the shipment was not seized in order to protect his cover. According to the Relatives for Justice pamphlet, between 1988 and June 1993 weapons from this shipment have reportedly been used in 63 killings (Relatives for Justice, Shoot-to-kill and Collusion, June 1993). A BBC Inside Ulster program, broadcast in January 1993, stated that the South African weapons greatly enhanced the killing capacity of Loyalist paramilitaries because of the sophistication of the weaponry.

11 London-based British Irish Rights Watch has documented such allegations in a report, Defending the Defenders, published in 1993. See also a Helsinki Watch Report, Human Rights in Northern Ireland, October 1991; and Human Rights and Legal Defense in Northern Ireland, a report published in February 1993 by the Lawyers Committee for Human Rights.

12 Fenian is a term applied to Catholics by Loyalists, the implication being that all Catholics are disloyal to the State and are therefore enemies.

13 BBC Panorama program, June 1992.

14 An interview with the RUC Chief Constable was published in the Belfast Telegraph, 22 September 1993.

15 One should also note that in a letter dated 23 September 1993 from Chief Constable John Stevens to British Irish Rights Watch, John Stevens stated: "I can confirm that the inquiry is still ongoing and all allegations are being thoroughly investigated, including the circumstances surrounding the murder of Patrick Finucane. I assure you that the inquiry will be both independent and impartial."

16 Newspaper reports show that security documents were found in June 1990 in a Loyalist area in Londonderry; that the RUC reported the loss of a photomontage with details on 38 suspects in the Tyrone area in December 1990; military intelligence files containing dozens of photographs went missing in South Armagh in July 1991; 15 people in Belfast were told in May 1992 that Loyalist paramilitaries held security information regarding them; British Army documents containing photographs and details of alleged IRA and Sinn Féin members in Co. Tyrone were found in a house in Belfast on 3 November 1993. In September 1992 the local newspaper Antrim Guardian was sent a copy of an intelligence document containing details on 20 people. One of them was Danny Cassidy, who had been killed in April 1992 (see page 44 of this document).

17 Relatives for Justice, Shoot-to-kill and Collusion, July 1993.

18 Sinn Féin is a legal political party which fields candidates in local and national elections; it is widely considered to be the political wing of the IRA.

19 The Social Democratic and Labour Party (SDLP) gets most of its support from the Catholic community. The main constitutional political parties which get most of their support from the Protestant community are the Ulster Democratic Unionist Party and the Ulster Unionist Party. In addition, the Ulster Alliance Party draws support from both communities.

20 93 per cent of the RUC is from the Protestant community.

21 The authorities have regularly cited official statistics comparing the numbers of Loyalists and Republicans imprisoned for serious crimes. Further research, however, is required to identify, among other things, whether there is any difference between the clear-up rates for purely sectarian murders by Loyalist groups and those for murders of targeted Republican suspects who were wanted or were under close surveillance by the security forces.

22 A television documentary entitled "The Forgotten Massacre" by the First Tuesday program on the British network ITV, screened in July 1993, claimed that soldiers in the British Army had helped to carry out bombings in May 1974 in Dublin during which 28 people were killed and 100 seriously injured and in Monaghan, also in the Irish Republic, in which five people were killed. Responsibility for the bomb-

ings was claimed in the name of the UVF. It was alleged that the investigation by British authorities into the alleged involvement of Northern Ireland groups or security force personnel in these bombings had not been carried out thoroughly.

23 Screened on television in October 1991, the program entitled "The Committee" alleged widespread collusion between the security forces, prominent members of the Loyalist community, and paramilitaries. After the screening of the program, Channel Four was ordered, under the Prevention of Terrorism Act, to disclose the name of their key source, which they refused to do on the grounds that such disclosure might expose him to murder. Channel Four was eventually fined £75,000 for failing to identify their source. Individual program makers were also subjected to investigation, including researcher Ben Hamilton, against whom perjury charges were eventually dropped.

24 The UDA was founded in 1971 as a co-ordinating body for Loyalist vigilante groups, many of them calling themselves "Defence Associations".

25 A survey among children aged 10 and 11 in Northern Ireland found that almost 20 per cent have been in or near a bomb explosion (Independent, 21 September 1992)

26 Irish Times, 7 December 1991.

27 Observer, 28 March 1993.

28 Article by Tony Horwitz, The Wall Street Journal, 7 July 1993.

Amnesty International is a worldwide voluntary movement that works to prevent some of the gravest violations by governments of people's fundamental human rights. The main focus of its campaigning is to:

- *free all prisoners of conscience.* These are people detained anywhere for their beliefs or because of their ethnic origin, sex, colour or language - who have not used or advocated violence.
- *ensure fair and prompt trials for political prisoners.*
- *abolish the death penalty, torture and other cruel treatment of prisoners.*
- *end extrajudicial executions and "disappearances".*

Amnesty International also opposes abuses by opposition groups: hostage taking, torture and killings of prisoners and other arbitrary killings.

Amnesty International, recognising that human rights are indivisible and interdependent, works to promote all the human rights enshrined in the Universal Declaration of Human Rights and other international standards, through human rights education programmes and campaigning for ratification of human rights treaties.

Amnesty International is impartial. It is independent of any government, political persuasion or religious creed. It does not support or oppose any government or political system, nor does it support or oppose the views of the victims whose rights it seeks to protect. It is concerned solely with the protection of the human rights involved in each case, regardless of the ideology of the government, opposition forces of the beliefs of the individual.

Amnesty International does not grade countries according to their record on human rights; instead of attempting comparisons it concentrates on trying to end the specific violations of human rights in each case.

Amnesty International has more than 1,100,000 members, subscribers and regular donors in over 150 countries and territories, with over 8000 local groups in over 70 countries in Africa, the Americas, Asia, Europe and the Middle East. To ensure impartiality, each group works on cases and campaigns in countries other than its own, selected fro geographical and political diversity. Research into human rights violations and individual victims is conducted by the International Secretariat of Amnesty International. No section, group or member is expected to provide information on their own country, and no section group or member has any responsibility for action taken or statements issued by the international organisation concerning their own country.

Amnesty International has formal relations with the United Nations Economic and Social Council (ECOSOC); the United Nations Educational, Scientific and Cultural Organisation (UNESCO); the Council of Europe; the Organisation of American States; the Organisation of African Unity and the Inter-Parliamentary Union.